Poems

Poems

Charles Dickens

Edited with commentaries
by F.G. Kitton

ALMA CLASSICS

ALMA CLASSICS
an imprint of

ALMA BOOKS LTD
3 Castle Yard
Richmond
Surrey TW10 6TF
United Kingdom
www.almaclassics.com

Poems first published as *The Poems and Verses of Charles Dickens* in 1903
First published by Alma Classics in 2013
This paperback edition first published by Alma Classics in 2016

Extra Material © Alma Classics

Printed in Great Britain by CPI Group (UK) Ltd, Croydon CR0 4YY

ISBN: 978-1-84749-690-4

Contents

Charles Dickens (1812–70)

Poems

Songs, Choruses and
Concerted Pieces from
The Village Coquettes,
a Comic Opera
1836

About the year 1834, when the earliest of the *Sketches by Boz* were appearing in print, a young composer named John Hullah set to music a portion of an opera called *The Gondolier*, which he thought might prove successful on the stage. Twelve months later Hullah became acquainted with Charles Dickens, whose name was then unknown to those outside his own immediate circle, and it occurred to him that he and "Boz" might combine their forces by converting *The Gondolier* into a popular play. Dickens, who always entertained a passion for the theatre, entered into the project at once, and informed Hullah that he had a little unpublished story by him which he thought would dramatize well – even better than *The Gondolier* notion; confessing that he would rather deal with familiar English scenes than with the unfamiliar Venetian environment of the play favoured by Hullah. The title of *The Gondolier* was consequently abandoned, and a novel subject found and put forward as *The Village Coquettes*, a comic opera of which songs, duets and concerted pieces were to form constituent parts. Dickens, of course, became responsible for the libretto and Hullah for the music; and when completed the little play was offered to, and accepted by, Braham, the lessee of the St James's Theatre, who expressed an earnest desire to be the first to introduce "Boz" to the public as a dramatic writer. A favourite comedian of that day, John Pritt Harley, after reading the words of the opera prior to its representation, declared it was "a sure card" and felt so confident of its success that he offered to wager ten pounds that it would run fifty nights! – an assurance which at once decided Braham to produce it.

The Village Coquettes, described on the title page of the printed copies as "A Comic Opera, in Two Acts", was played for the first time on 6th December 1836, with Braham and Harley in the cast. In his preface to the play (published contemporaneously by Richard Bentley, and dedicated to Harley) Dickens explained that "the libretto of an opera must be, to a certain extent, a mere vehicle for the music", and that "it is scarcely fair or reasonable to judge it by those strict rules of criticism which would be justly applicable to a five-act tragedy or a finished comedy". There is no doubt that the merits of the play were based upon the songs set to Hullah's music rather than upon the play itself, and it is said that Harley's reputation as a vocalist was established by his able rendering of them.

The Village Coquettes enjoyed a run of nineteen nights in London during the season, and was then transferred to Edinburgh, where it was performed under the management of Mr Ramsay, a friend of Sir Walter Scott. Sala, as a boy of ten, witnessed its first representation in London, and ever retained a vivid impression of the event; while especial interest appertains to the fact that a copy of the play became the means of first bringing Dickens into personal communication with John Forster, his lifelong friend and biographer. It is more than probable that "Boz" felt a little elated by the reception accorded by the public to the "dramatic bantling" but as time progressed he realized that the somewhat unfavourable comments of the critics were not entirely devoid of truth. Indeed, when in 1843 it was proposed to revive the play, he expressed a hope that it might be allowed "to sink into its native obscurity". "I did it," he explained, "in a fit of damnable good nature long ago, for Hullah, who wrote some very pretty music to it. I just put down for everybody what everybody at the St James's Theatre wanted to say and do, and what they could say and do best, and I have been most sincerely repentant ever since." The novelist confessed that both the operetta and a little farce called *The Strange Gentleman* (the latter written as "a practical joke" for the St James's Theatre about the same time) were done "without the least consideration or regard to reputation"; he also declared that he "wouldn't repeat them for a thousand pounds apiece", and devoutly wished these early dramatic efforts to be forgotten. Apropos of this, the late Frederick Locker-Lampson has recorded that when he asked Dickens (about a year before the great writer's death) whether he possessed a copy of *The Village Coquettes*, his reply was "No; and if I knew it was in my house, and if I could not get rid of it in any other way, I would burn the wing of the house where it was!"

Although, perhaps, not of a high order of merit, *The Village Coquettes* is not without bibliographical interest, and may be regarded as a musical and literary curiosity. Copies of the first edition of the little play are now seldom met with, and whenever a perfect impression comes into the market it commands a good price, even as much as ten or twelve pounds – indeed, a particularly fine copy was sold at Sotheby's in 1889 for twenty-five pounds. In 1878 the words of the opera were reprinted in facsimile by Richard Bentley, for which a frontispiece was etched by F. W. Pailthorpe a year later.

Round

Hail to the merry autumn days, when yellow cornfields shine,
Far brighter than the costly cup that holds the monarch's wine!
Hail to the merry harvest time, the gayest of the year,
The time of rich and bounteous crops, rejoicing and good cheer!

'Tis pleasant on a fine spring morn to see the buds expand,
'Tis pleasant in the summertime to view the teeming land;
'Tis pleasant on a winter's night to crouch around the blaze –
But what are joys like these, my boys, to autumn's merry days!

Then hail to merry autumn days, when yellow cornfields shine,
Far brighter than the costly cup that holds the monarch's wine!
And hail to merry harvest time, the gayest of the year,
The time of rich and bounteous crops, rejoicing and good cheer!

Lucy's Song

Love is not a feeling to pass away,
Like the balmy breath of a summer day;
It is not – it cannot be – laid aside;
It is not a thing to forget or hide.
It clings to the heart, ah, woe is me!
As the ivy clings to the old oak tree.

Love is not a passion of earthly mould,
As a thirst for honour, or fame, or gold;
For when all these wishes have died away,
The deep, strong love of a brighter day,
Though nourished in secret, consumes the more,
As the slow rust eats to the iron's core.

Squire Norton's Song

That very wise head, old Aesop, said,
The bow should be sometimes loose;
Keep it tight for ever, the string you sever –
Let's turn his old moral to use.
The world forget, and let us yet,
The glass our spirits buoying,
Revel tonight in those moments bright
Which make life worth enjoying.

    CHORUS – The cares of the day, old moralists say,
    Are quite enough to perplex one;
    Then drive today's sorrow away till tomorrow,
    And then put it off till the next one.

Some plodding old crones – the heartless drones!
Appeal to my cool reflection,
And ask me whether such nights can ever
Charm sober recollection.
Yes, yes! I cry, I'll grieve and die,
When those I love forsake me;
But while friends so dear surround me here,
Let Care, if he can, o'ertake me.

    CHORUS – The cares of the day, etc.

George Edmunds's Song

Autumn leaves, autumn leaves, lie strewn around me here;
Autumn leaves, autumn leaves, how sad, how cold, how drear!
    How like the hopes of childhood's day,
    Thick clust'ring on the bough!
    How like those hopes in their decay –
    How faded are they now!
Autumn leaves, autumn leaves, lie strewn around me here;
Autumn leaves, autumn leaves, how sad, how cold, how drear!

Wither'd leaves, wither'd leaves, that fly before the gale:
Withered leaves, withered leaves, ye tell a mournful tale,
    Of love once true, and friends once kind,
    And happy moments fled:
    Dispersed by every breath of wind,
    Forgotten, changed or dead!
Autumn leaves, autumn leaves, lie strewn around me here!
Autumn leaves, autumn leaves, how sad, how cold, how drear!

Rose's Song

Some folks who have grown old and sour,
Say love does nothing but annoy.
   The fact is, they have had their hour,
So envy what they can't enjoy.
I like the glance – I like the sigh –
   That does of ardent passion tell!
If some folks were as young as I,
   I'm sure they'd like it quite as well.

Old maiden aunts so hate the men,
   So well know how wives are harried,
It makes them sad – not jealous – when
   They see their poor, dear nieces married.
All men are fair and false, they know,
   And with deep sighs they assail 'em;
It's so long since they tried men, though,
   I rather think their mem'ries fail 'em.

Duet (Flam and Rose)

FLAM   'Tis true I'm caressed by the witty,
      The envy of all the fine beaux,
    The pet of the court and the city,
      But still, I'm the lover of Rose.

ROSE   Country sweethearts, oh, how I despise!
      And oh! How delighted I am
    To think that I shine in the eyes
      Of the elegant – sweet – Mr Flam.

FLAM   Allow me (*offers to kiss her*).

ROSE   Pray don't be so bold, sir (*kisses her*).

FLAM   What sweets on that honey'd lip hang!

ROSE   Your presumption, I know, I should scold, sir,
      But I really can't scold Mr Flam –

BOTH   Then let us be happy together,
      Content with the world as it goes,
    An unchangeable couple for ever,
      Mr Flam and his beautiful Rose.

Squire Norton's Song

The child and the old man sat alone
   In the quiet, peaceful shade
Of the old green boughs that had richly grown
   In the deep, thick forest glade.
It was a soft and pleasant sound,
   That rustling of the oak;
And the gentle breeze played lightly round,
   As thus the fair boy spoke:

"Dear father, what can honour be,
   Of which I hear men rave?
Field, cell and cloister, land and sea,
   The tempest and the grave:
It lives in all, 'tis sought in each,
   'Tis never heard or seen:
Now tell me, father, I beseech,
   What can this honour mean?"

"It is a name – a name, my child –
   It lived in other days,
When men were rude, their passions wild,
   Their sport, thick battle frays.

When, in armour bright, the warrior bold
  Knelt to his lady's eyes:
Beneath the abbey pavement old
  That warrior's dust now lies.

"The iron hearts of that old day
  Have mouldered in the grave;
And chivalry has passed away,
  With knights so true and brave;
The honour, which to them was life,
  Throbs in no bosom now;
It only gilds the gambler's strife,
  Or decks the worthless vow."

Duet (The Squire and Lucy)

SQUIRE   In rich and lofty station shine,
              Before his jealous eyes;
              In golden splendour, lady mine,
              This peasant youth despise.

LUCY (*apart; the Squire regarding her attentively*)
              Oh! It would be revenge indeed,
              With scorn his glance to meet.
              I, I, his humble pleading heed!
              I'd spurn him from my feet.

SQUIRE   With love and rage her bosom's torn,
              And rash the choice will be;
LUCY   With love and rage my bosom's torn,
              And rash the choice will be.

SQUIRE   From hence she quickly most be borne,
              Her home, her home, she'll flee.
LUCY   Oh! Long shall I have cause to mourn
              My home, my home, for thee!

Sestet and Chorus

YOUNG BENSON   Turn him from the farm! From his home will you cast
        The old man who has tilled it for years!
    Ev'ry tree, ev'ry flower, is linked with the past,
        And a friend of his childhood appears.
    Turn *him* from the farm! O'er its grassy hillside,
        A gay boy he once loved to range;
    His boyhood has fled, and its dear friends are dead,
        But these meadows have never known change.

EDMUNDS   Oppressor, hear me!

LUCY   On my knees I implore.

SQUIRE   I command it, and you will obey.

ROSE   Rise, dear Lucy, rise; you shall not kneel before
        The tyrant who drives us away.

SQUIRE   Your sorrows are useless, your prayers are in vain:
        I command it, and you will begone.
    I'll hear no more.

EDMUNDS   No, they shall not beg again
    Of a man whom I view with deep scorn.

FLAM   Do not yield.

YOUNG BENSON
SQUIRE
LUCY   }   Leave the farm!
ROSE

18

EDMUNDS	Your pow'r I despise.
SQUIRE	And your threats, boy, I disregard too.
FLAM	Do not yield.
YOUNG BENSON	
SQUIRE	
LUCY	Leave the farm!
ROSE	

ROSE	If he leaves it, he dies.
EDMUNDS	This base act, proud man, you shall rue.
YOUNG BENSON	Turn him from the farm! From his home will you cast

> The old man who has tilled it for years?
> Ev'ry tree, ev'ry flower, is linked with the past,
> And a friend of his childhood appears!

SQUIRE Yes, yes, leave the farm! From his home I will cast
> The old man who has tilled it for years;
> Though each tree and flower is linked with the past,
> And a friend of his childhood appears.

CHORUS

He has turned from his farm! From his home he has cast
> The old man who has tilled it for years;
> Though each tree and flower is linked with the past,
> And a friend of his childhood appears.

Quartet

SQUIRE   Hear me, when I swear that the farm is your own
              Through all changes Fortune may make;
              The base charge of falsehood I never have known;
              This promise I never will break.

ROSE }   Hear him, when he swears that the farm is our own
LUCY   Through all changes Fortune may make.

ROSE }   The base charge of falsehood he never has known;
LUCY   This promise he never will break.

(*Enter Young Benson.*)

YOUNG BENSON My sister here! Lucy! begone, I command.

SQUIRE   To your home I restore you again.

YOUNG BENSON No boon I'll accept from that treacherous hand
              As the price of my fair sister's fame.

SQUIRE   To your home!

YOUNG BENSON (*to Lucy*) Hence away!

LUCY   Brother dear, I obey.

SQUIRE   I restore.

YOUNG BENSON   Hence away!

YOUNG BENSON }
ROSE   Let us leave.
LUCY   }

LUCY	He swears it, dear brother.
SQUIRE	I swear it.
YOUNG BENSON	Away!
SQUIRE	I swear it.
YOUNG BENSON	You swear to deceive.
SQUIRE	Hear me, when I swear that the farm is your own Through all changes Fortune may make.
LUCY } ROSE }	Hear him, when he swears that the farm is our own Through all changes Fortune may make.
YOUNG BENSON	Hear him swear, hear him swear, that the farm is our own Through all changes Fortune may make.
SQUIRE	The base charge of falsehood I never have known, This promise I never will break.
LUCY } ROSE }	The base charge of falsehood he never has known, This promise he never will break.
YOUNG BENSON	The base charge of falsehood he often has known, This promise he surely will break.

Squire Norton's Song

There's a charm in spring, when ev'rything
  Is bursting from the ground;
When pleasant show'rs bring forth the flow'rs
  And all is life around.

In summer day, the fragrant hay
  Most sweetly scents the breeze;
And all is still, save murm'ring rill,
  Or sound of humming bees.

Old autumn comes; with trusty gun
  In quest of birds we roam:
Unerring aim, we mark the game,
  And proudly bear it home.

A winter's night has its delight,
  Well warmed to bed we go:
A winter's day, we're blithe and gay,
  Snipe-shooting in the snow.

A country life, without the strife
　And noisy din of town,
Is all I need, I take no heed
　Of splendour or renown.

And when I die, oh, let me lie
　Where trees above me wave;
Let wild plants bloom around my tomb,
　My quiet country grave!

Young Benson's Song

My fair home is no longer mine;
  From its roof-tree I'm driven away.
Alas! Who will tend the old vine,
  Which I planted in infancy's day?
The garden, the beautiful flowers,
  The oak with its branches on high,
Dear friends of my happiest hours,
  Among thee I long hoped to die.
The briar, the moss and the bramble,
  Along the green paths will run wild:
The paths where I once used to ramble,
  An innocent, light-hearted child.

Duet (The Squire and Edmunds)

SQUIRE   Listen, though I do not fear you,
Listen to me, ere we part.

EDMUNDS   List to you! Yes, I will hear you.

SQUIRE   Yours alone is Lucy's heart,
I swear it, by that Heav'n above me.

EDMUNDS   What! can I believe my ears!
Could I hope that she still loves me!

SQUIRE   Banish all these doubts and fears,
If a love were e'er worth gaining,
If love were ever fond and true,
No disguise or passion feigning,
Such is her young love for you.

SQUIRE   Listen, though I do not fear you,
Listen to me, ere we part.

EDMUNDS   List to you! Yes, I will hear you,
Mine alone is her young heart.

Lucy's Song

How beautiful at eventide
 To see the twilight shadows pale,
Steal o'er the landscape, far and wide,
 O'er stream and meadow, mound and dale!
How soft is Nature's calm repose
 When ev'ning skies their cool dews weep:
The gentlest wind more gently blows,
 As if to soothe her in her sleep!
  The gay morn breaks,
   Mists roll away,
  All Nature awakes
   To glorious day.
  In my breast alone
   Dark shadows remain;
  The peace it has known
   It can never regain.

Join the dance, with step as light
As ev'ry heart should be tonight;
Music, shake the lofty dome,
In honour of our Harvest Home.

Join the dance, and banish care,
All are young, and gay, and fair;
Even age has youthful grown,
In honour of our Harvest Home.

Join the dance, bright faces beam,
Sweet lips smile, and dark eyes gleam;
All these charms have hither come,
In honour of our Harvest Home.

Join the dance, with step as light,
As ev'ry heart should be tonight;
Music shake the lofty dome
In honour of our Harvest Home.

Quintet

No light bound
Of stag or timid hare,
   O'er the ground
Where startled herds repair,
   Do we prize
So high, or hold so dear,
   As the eyes
That light our pleasures here.
   No cool breeze
That gently plays by night,
   O'er calm seas,
Whose waters glisten bright;
   No soft moan
That sighs across the lea,
   Harvest Home,
Is half so sweet as thee!

Lyric from
The Lamplighter,
a Farce
1838

In 1838 Dickens agreed to prepare a little play for Macready, the famous actor, then the manager of Drury Lane Theatre. It was called *The Lamplighter*, and when completed the author read aloud the "unfortunate little farce" (as he subsequently termed it) in the green room of the theatre. Although the play went through rehearsal, it was never presented before an audience, for the actors would not agree about it, and, at Macready's suggestion, Dickens consented to withdraw it, declaring that he had "no other feeling of disappointment connected with this matter" but that which arose from the failure in attempting to serve his friend. The manuscript of the play, not in Dickens's handwriting, reposes in the Forster Library at the Victoria and Albert Museum, and in 1879 it was printed for the first time, in the form of a pamphlet, of which only two hundred and fifty copies were issued.

When rejected by Macready as unsuitable for stage presentation, *The Lamplighter* was adapted by Dickens to another purpose – that is to say, he converted it into a tale called 'The Lamplighter's Story'," for publication in *The Pic-Nic Papers*, issued in 1841 for the benefit of the widow of Macrone, Dickens's first publisher, who died in great poverty. Between the farce and the story there are but slight differences. The duet of two verses, sung by Tom and Betsy to the air of 'The Young May Moon', cannot, of course, be regarded as a remarkable composition, but it served its purpose sufficiently well, and for that reason deserves recognition.

Duet from *The Lamplighter*
(Air – 'The Young May Moon')

TOM   There comes a new moon twelve times a year.

BETSY   And when there is none, all is dark and drear.

TOM   In which I espy—

BETSY   And so, too, do I—

BOTH   A resemblance to womankind very clear—

BOTH   There comes a new moon twelve times a year;
And when there is none, all is dark and drear.

TOM   In which I espy—

BETSY   And so do I—

BOTH   A resemblance to womankind very clear.

TOM   She changes, she's fickle, she drives men mad.

BETSY   She comes to bring light, and leaves them sad.

TOM   So restless wild—

BETSY   But so sweetly wild—

BOTH   That no better companion could be had.

BOTH   There comes a new moon twelve times a year;
And when there is none, all is dark and drear.

TOM   In which I espy—

BETSY   And so do I—

BOTH   A resemblance to womankind very clear.

Songs from
The Pickwick Papers
1837

The Ivy Green

This famous ballad of three verses, from the sixth chapter of *Pickwick*, is perhaps the most acceptable of all Dickens's poetical efforts. It was originally set to music, at Dickens's request, by his brother-in-law, Henry Burnett, a professional vocalist, who, by the way, was the admitted prototype of Nicholas Nickleby. Mr Burnett sang the ballad scores of times in the presence of literary men and artists, and it proved an especial favourite with Landor. 'The Ivy Green' was not written for *Pickwick*, Mr Burnett assured me; but on its being so much admired the author said it should go into a monthly number, and it did. The most popular setting is undoubtedly that of Henry Russell, who has recorded that he received, as his fee, the magnificent sum of ten shillings! The ballad, in this form, went into many editions, and the sales must have amounted to tens of thousands.

The Ivy Green

Oh, a dainty plant is the Ivy green,
  That creepeth o'er ruins old!
Of right choice food are his meals, I ween,
  In his cell so lone and cold.
The wall must be crumbled, the stone decayed,
  To pleasure his dainty whim:
And the mouldering dust that years have made
  Is a merry meal for him.
    Creeping where no life is seen,
    A rare old plant is the Ivy green.

Fast he stealeth on, though he wears no wings,
  And a stanch old heart has he.
How closely he twineth, how tight he clings,
  To his friend the huge Oak Tree!
And slyly he traileth along the ground,
  And his leaves he gently waves,
As he joyously hugs and crawleth round
  The rich mould of dead men's graves.
    Creeping where grim death hath been,
    A rare old plant is the Ivy green.

Whole ages have fled and their works decayed,
  And nations have scattered been;
But the stout old Ivy shall never fade,
  From its hale and hearty green.
The brave old plant, in its lonely days,
  Shall fatten upon the past:
For the stateliest building man can raise
  Is the Ivy's food at last.
    Creeping on, where time has been,
    A rare old plant is the Ivy green.

A Christmas Carol

The five stanzas bearing the above title will be found in the twenty-eighth chapter of *Pickwick*, where they are introduced as the song which that hospitable old soul, Mr Wardle, sung appropriately, "in a good, round, sturdy voice", before the Pickwickians and others assembled on Christmas Eve at Manor Farm. The 'Carol', shortly after its appearance in *Pickwick*, was set to music to the air of 'Old King Cole', and published in *The Book of British Song* (new edition), with an illustration drawn by "Alfred Crowquill" – i.e. A.H. Forrester.

A Christmas Carol

I care not for spring; on his fickle wing
   Let the blossoms and buds be borne:
He woos them amain with his treacherous rain,
   And he scatters them ere the morn.
An inconstant elf, he knows not himself
   Nor his own changing mind an hour,
He'll smile in your face, and, with wry grimace,
   He'll wither your youngest flower.

Let the summer sun to his bright home run,
   He shall never be sought by me;
When he's dimmed by a cloud I can laugh aloud,
   And care not how sulky he be!
For his darling child is the madness wild
   That sports in fierce fever's train;
And when love is too strong, it don't last long,
   As many have found to their pain.

A mild harvest night, by the tranquil light
   Of the modest and gentle moon,
Has a far sweeter sheen, for me, I ween,
   Than the broad and unblushing noon.

But every leaf awakens my grief,
   As it lieth beneath the tree;
So let autumn air be never so fair,
   It by no means agrees with me.

But my song I troll out, for Christmas stout,
   The hearty, the true, and the bold;
A bumper I drain, and with might and main
   Give three cheers for this Christmas old!
We'll usher him in with a merry din
   That shall gladden his joyous heart.
And we'll keep him up, while there's bite or sup,
   And in fellowship good we'll part.

In his fine, honest pride, he scorns to hide
   One jot of his hard-weather scars;
They're no disgrace, for there's much the same trace
   On the cheeks of our bravest tars.
Then again I sing, till the roof doth ring,
   And it echoes from wall to wall –
To the stout old wight, fair welcome tonight,
   As the King of the Seasons all!

Gabriel Grub's Song

The Sexton's melancholy dirge, in the twenty-ninth chapter of *Pickwick*, seems a little incongruous in a humorous work. The sentiment, however, thoroughly accords with the philosophic grave-digger's gruesome occupation. 'The Story of the Goblins who Stole a Sexton' is one of several short tales (chiefly of a dismal character) introduced into *Pickwick*; they were doubtless written prior to the conception of *Pickwick*, each being probably intended for independent publication, and in a manner similar to the "Boz" Sketches. For some reason these stories were not so published, and Dickens evidently saw a favourable opportunity of utilizing his unused manuscripts by inserting them in *The Pickwick Papers*.

Gabriel Grub's Song

Brave lodgings for one, brave lodgings for one,
A few feet of cold earth, when life is done;
A stone at the head, a stone at the feet,
A rich, juicy meal for the worms to eat;
Rank grass overhead, and damp clay around,
Brave lodgings for one, these, in holy ground!

Romance

It will be remembered that while Sam Weller and his coaching friends refreshed themselves at the little public house opposite the Insolvent Court in Portugal Street, Lincoln's Inn Fields, prior to Sam joining Mr Pickwick in the Fleet, that faithful body servant was persuaded to "oblige the company" with a song. "Raly, gentlemen," said Sam, "I'm not wery much in the habit o' singin' vithout the instrument; but anythin' for a quiet life, as the man said ven he took the sitivation at the lighthouse."

With this prelude, Mr Samuel Weller burst at once into the following wild and beautiful legend, which, under the impression that it is not generally known, we take the liberty of quoting. We would beg to call particular attention to the monosyllable at the end of the second and fourth lines, which not only enables the singer to take breath at those points, but greatly assists the metre.

– *The Pickwick Papers*, Chapter 43

At the conclusion of the performance the mottled-faced gentleman contended that the song was "personal to the cloth", and demanded the name of the bishop's coachman, whose cowardice he regarded as a reflection upon coachmen in general. Sam replied that his name was not known, as "he hadn't got his card in his pocket"; whereupon the mottled-faced gentleman declared the statement to be untrue, stoutly maintaining that the said coachman did *not* run away, but "died game – game as pheasants", and he would "hear nothin' said to the contrairey".

Even in the vernacular (observes Mr Percy Fitzgerald), "this master of words [Charles Dickens] could be artistic; and it may fairly be asserted that Mr Weller's song to the coachmen is superior to anything of the kind that has appeared since". The two stanzas have been set to music, as a humorous part-song, by Sir Frederick Bridge, Mus. Doc., MVO, the organist of Westminster Abbey, who informs me that it was written some years since, to celebrate a festive gathering in honour of Dr Turpin (!), Secretary of the College of Organists. "It has had a very great success," says Sir Frederick, "and is sung much in the north of England at competitions of choirs. It is for men's voices. The humour of the words never fails to make a great hit, and I hope the music does no harm. 'The Bishop's Coach' is set to a bit of old plainchant, and I introduce a fugue at the words 'Sure as eggs is eggs'."

Romance

I

Bold Turpin vunce, on Hounslow Heath,
  His bold mare Bess bestrode-er;
Ven there he see'd the Bishop's coach
  A-comin' along the road-er.
So he gallops close to the 'orse's legs,
  And he claps his head vithin;
And the Bishop says, "Sure as eggs is eggs,
  This here's the bold Turpin!"

CHORUS

And the Bishop says, "Sure as eggs is eggs,
  This here's the bold Turpin!"

II

Says Turpin, "You shall eat your words,
  With a sarse of leaden bul-let";
So he puts a pistol to his mouth,
  And he fires it down his gul-let.
The coachman, he not likin' the job,
  Set off at a full gal-lop,

But Dick put a couple of balls in his nob,
 And perwailed on him to stop.

CHORUS (*sarcastically*)
But Dick put a couple of balls in his nob,
And perwailed on him to stop.

Political Squibs from
The Examiner
1841

In August 1841, Dickens contributed anonymously to *The Examiner* (then edited by Forster) three political squibs, which were signed W. and were intended to help the Liberals in fighting their opponents. These squibs were entitled respectively 'The Fine Old English Gentleman (To Be Said or Sung at All Conservative Dinners)'; 'The Quack Doctor's Proclamation'; and 'Subjects for Painters (after Peter Pindar)'. Concerning those productions, Forster says: "I doubt if he ever enjoyed anything more than the power of thus taking part occasionally, unknown to outsiders, in the sharp conflict the press was waging at the time." In all probability he contributed other political rhymes to the pages of *The Examiner* as events prompted: if so, they are buried beyond easy reach of identification.

Writing to Forster at this time, Dickens said: "By Jove, how Radical I am getting! I wax stronger and stronger in the true principles every day." He would (observes Forster) sometimes even talk, in moments of sudden indignation at the political outlook, "of carrying off himself and his household gods, like Coriolanus, to a world elsewhere". This was the period of the Tory interregnum, with Sir Robert Peel at the head of affairs.

The Fine Old English Gentleman
New Version
(To Be Said or Sung at All Conservative Dinners)

I'll sing you a new ballad, and I'll warrant it first-rate,
Of the days of that old gentleman who had that old estate;
When they spent the public money at a bountiful old rate
On ev'ry mistress, pimp and scamp, at ev'ry noble gate,
   In the fine old English Tory times;
   Soon may they come again!

The good old laws were garnished well with gibbets, whips and chains,
With fine old English penalties, and fine old English pains,
With rebel heads, and seas of blood once hot in rebel veins;
For all these things were requisite to guard the rich old gains
   Of the fine old English Tory times;
   Soon may they come again!

This brave old code, like Argus,* had a hundred watchful eyes,
And ev'ry English peasant had his good old English spies,
To tempt his starving discontent with fine old English lies,
Then call the good old Yeomanry to stop his peevish cries,
   In the fine old English Tory times;
   Soon may they come again!

The good old times for cutting throats that cried out in their need,
The good old times for hunting men who held their fathers' creed,
The good old times when William Pitt,* as all good men agreed,
Came down direct from Paradise at more than railroad speed...
  Oh, the fine old English Tory times;
  When will they come again!

In those rare days, the press was seldom known to snarl or bark,
But sweetly sang of men in pow'r, like any tuneful lark;
Grave judges, too, to all their evil deeds were in the dark;
And not a man in twenty score knew how to make his mark.
  Oh, the fine old English Tory times;
  Soon may they come again!

Those were the days for taxes, and for war's infernal din;
For scarcity of bread, that fine old dowagers might win;
For shutting men of letters up, through iron bars to grin,
Because they didn't think the Prince was altogether thin.
  In the fine old English Tory times;
  Soon may they come again!

But tolerance, though slow in flight, is strong-wing'd in the main;
That night must come on these fine days, in course of time was plain;
The pure old spirit struggled, but its struggles were in vain;
A nation's grip was on it, and it died in choking pain,
  With the fine old English Tory days,
  All of the olden time.

The bright old day now dawns again; the cry runs through the land,
In England there shall be dear bread – in Ireland, sword and brand;
And poverty and ignorance shall swell the rich and grand,
So, rally round the rulers with the gentle iron hand,
  Of the fine old English Tory days;
  Hail to the coming time!

W.

The Quack Doctor's Proclamation
(Tune – 'A Cobbler There Was')

An astonishing doctor has just come to town,
Who will do all the faculty perfectly brown:
He knows all diseases, their causes and ends;
And he begs to appeal to his medical friends.
    Tol de rol:
    Diddle doll:
  Tol de rol, de dol,
    Diddle doll
    Tol de rol doll.

He's a magnetic doctor, and knows how to keep
The whole of a government snoring asleep
To popular clamours; till popular pins
Are stuck in their midriffs – and then he begins
    Tol de rol.

He's a *clairvoyant* subject, and readily reads
His countrymen's wishes, condition and needs,
With many more fine things I can't tell in rhyme –
And he keeps both his eyes shut the whole of the time.
    Tol de rol.

You mustn't expect him to talk; but you'll take
Most particular notice the doctor's awake,
Though for aught from his words or his looks that you reap, he
Might just as well be most confoundedly sleepy.
    Tol de rol.

Homoeopathy, too, he has practised for ages
(You'll find his prescriptions in Luke Hansard's pages),
Just giving his patient when maddened by pain –
Of reform the ten-thousandth part of a grain.
    Tol de rol.

He's a med'cine for Ireland, in portable papers;
The infallible cure for political vapours;
A neat label round it his 'prentices tie –
"Put your trust in the Lord, and keep this powder dry!"
    Tol de rol.

He's a corn doctor also, of wonderful skill –
No cutting, no rooting-up, purging or pill;
You're merely to take, 'stead of walking or riding,
The sweet schoolboy exercise – innocent sliding.
    Tol de rol.

There's no advice gratis. If high ladies send
His legitimate fee, he's their soft-spoken friend.
At the great public counter with one hand behind him,
And one in his waistcoat, they're certain to find him.
    Tol de rol.

He has only to add he's the real Doctor Flam,
All others being purely fictitious and sham;
The house is a large one, tall, slated and white,
With a lobby; and lights in the passage at night.

    Tol de rol:
    Diddle doll:
  Tol de rol, de dol,
    Diddle doll
    Tol de rol doll.

W.

Subjects for Painters
(After Peter Pindar)*

To you, Sir Martin,* and your co-RAs,
  I dedicate in meek, suggestive lays,
Some subjects for your academic palettes;
   Hoping, by dint of these my scanty jobs,
   To fill with novel thoughts your teeming nobs,
As though I beat them in with wooden mallets.

To you, Maclise,* who Eve's fair daughters paint
  With Nature's hand, and want the maudlin taint
Of the sweet Chalon* school of silk and ermine:
   To you, E. Landseer,* who from year to year
   Delight in beasts and birds, and dogs and deer,
And seldom give us any human vermin:
   To all who practise art, or make believe,
   I offer subjects they may take or leave.

Great Sibthorp* and his butler, in debate
  (*Arcades ambo*)* on affairs of state,
Not altogether "gone", but rather funny;
   Cursing the Whigs for leaving in the lurch

Our d—d good, pleasant, gentlemanly Church,
Would make a picture – cheap at any money.

Or Sibthorp as the Tory Sec.-at-War,
    Encouraging his mates with loud "Yhor! Yhor!"
From Treas'ry benches' most conspicuous end;
    Or Sib.'s mustachios curling with a smile,
    As an expectant premier without guile
Calls him his honourable and gallant friend.

Or Sibthorp travelling in foreign parts,
    Through that rich portion of our Eastern charts
Where lies the land of popular tradition;
    And fairly worshipp'd by the true devout
    In all his comings-in and goings-out,
Because of the old Turkish superstition.

Fame with her trumpet, blowing very hard,
    And making earth rich with celestial lard,
In puffing deeds done through Lord Chamberlain Howe;*
    While some few thousand persons of small gains,
    Who give their charities without such pains,
Look up, much wondering what may be the row.

Behind them Joseph Hume,* who turns his pate
    To where great Marlbro' House in princely state

Shelters a host of lackeys, lords and pages,
  And says he knows of dowagers a crowd,
  Who, without trumpeting so very loud,
Would do so much, and more, for half the wages.

  Limn, sirs, the highest lady in the land,
  When Joseph Surface,* fawning cap in hand,
Delivers in his list of patriot mortals;
  Those gentlemen of honour, faith and truth,
  Who, foul-mouthed, spat upon her maiden youth,
And doglike did defile her palace portals.

  Paint me the Tories, full of grief and woe,
  Weeping (to voters) over Frost* and Co.,
Their suff'ring, erring, much enduring brothers.
  And in the background don't forget to pack,
  Each grinning ghastly from its bloody sack,
The heads of Thistlewood, Despard* and others.

  Paint, squandering the club's election gold,
  Fierce lovers of our constitution old,
Lords who're that sacred lady's greatest debtors;
  And let the law, forbidding any voice
  Or act of peer to influence the choice
Of English people, flourish in bright letters.

Paint that same dear old lady, ill at ease,
Weak in her second childhood, hard to please,
Unknowing what she ails or what she wishes;
With all her Carlton nephews at the door,
Deaf'ning both aunt and nurses with their roar
— Fighting already for the loaves and fishes.
Leaving these hints for you to dwell upon,
I shall presume to offer more anon.

W.

Prologue to
Westland Marston's Play
The Patrician's Daughter
1842

The Patrician's Daughter was the title bestowed upon a play, in the tragic vein, by a then unknown writer, J. Westland Marston, it being his maiden effort in dramatic authorship. Dickens took great interest in the young man and indicated a desire to promote the welfare of his production by composing some introductory lines. To Macready he wrote: "The more I think of Marston's play, the more sure I feel that a prologue to the purpose would help it materially, and almost decide the fate of any ticklish point on the first night. Now I have an idea (not easily explainable in writing, but told in five words) that would take the prologue out of the conventional dress of prologues, quite. Get the curtain up with a dash, and begin the play with a sledge-hammer blow. If, on consideration, you should agree with me, I will write the prologue, heartily."

Happily for the author, his little tragedy was the first new play of the season, and it thus attracted greater attention. Its initial representation took place at Drury Lane Theatre, on 10th December 1842, and the fact that Dickens's dignified and vigorous lines were recited by Macready, the leading actor of his day, undoubtedly gave prestige to this performance; but the play, although it made a sensation for the moment, did not enjoy a long run, its motive being for some reason misunderstood. As explained by the editors of *The Letters of Charles Dickens*, it was (to a certain extent) an experiment in testing the effect of a tragedy of modern times and in modern dress, the novelist's prologue being intended to show that there need be no incongruity between plain clothes of the nineteenth century and high tragedy.

The Patrician's Daughter: A Tragedy in Five Acts appeared in pamphlet form during the year prior to its being placed upon the boards. The prologue was printed for the first time in the *Sunday Times*, 11th December 1842, and then in *The Theatrical Journal and Stranger's Guide*, 17th December 1842. By the kind permission of Miss Hogarth, the lines are here reproduced from the revised and only correct version in *The Letters of Charles Dickens*.

In the preface to the second edition of the play (1842), the author thus acknowledges his indebtedness to Dickens for the prologue, which, however, does not appear in the book: "How shall I thank Mr Dickens for the spontaneous kindness which has furnished me with so excellent a letter of introduction to the audience? The simplest acknowledgement is perhaps the best, since the least I might say would exceed *his* estimate of the obligation; while the most I could say would fail to express *mine*."

Prologue to
The Patrician's Daughter
(Spoken by Mr Macready)

No tale of streaming plumes and harness bright
Dwells on the poet's maiden harp tonight;
No trumpet's clamour and no battle's fire
Breathes in the trembling accents of his lyre;
Enough for him, if in his lowly strain
He wakes one household echo not in vain;
Enough for him, if in his boldest word
The beating heart of man be dimly heard.

Its solemn music which, like strains that sigh
Through charmed gardens, all who hearing die;
Its solemn music he does not pursue
To distant ages out of human view;
Nor listen to its wild and mournful chime
In the dead caverns on the shore of Time;
But musing with a calm and steady gaze
Before the crackling flames of living days,
He hears it whisper through the busy roar
Of what shall be and what has been before.
Awake the Present! Shall no scene display
The tragic passion of the passing day?

Is it with Man, as with some meaner things,
That out of death his single purpose springs
Can his eventful life no moral teach
Until he be, for aye, beyond its reach?
Obscurely shall he suffer, act and fade,
Dubb'd noble only by the sexton's spade?
Awake the Present! Though the steel-clad age
Find life alone within its storied page,
Iron is worn, at heart, by many still —
The tyrant Custom binds the serf-like will;
If the sharp rack, and screw, and chain be gone,
These later days have tortures of their own;
The guiltless writhe, while Guilt is stretch'd in sleep,
And Virtue lies, too often, dungeon deep.
Awake the Present! What the Past has sown
Be in its harvest garner'd, reap'd and grown!
How pride breeds pride, and wrong engenders wrong,
Read in the volume Truth has held so long,
Assured that where life's flowers freshest blow,
The sharpest thorns and keenest briars grow,
How social usage has the pow'r to change
Good thoughts to evil; in its highest range
To cramp the noble soul, and turn to ruth
The kindling impulse of our glorious youth,
Crushing the spirit in its house of clay,
Learn from the lessons of the present day.
Not light its import and not poor its mien;
Yourselves the actors, and your homes the scene.

A Word in Season,
from *The Keepsake*
1844

The Keepsake, one of the many fashionable annuals published during the early years of Queen Victoria's reign, had for its editor in 1844 the "gorgeous" Countess of Blessington, the reigning beauty who held court at Gore House, Kensington, where many political, artistic and literary celebrities foregathered – Bulwer Lytton, Disraeli, Dickens, Ainsworth, D'Orsay and the rest. Her Ladyship, through her personal charm and natural gifts, succeeded in securing the services of eminent authors for the aristocratic publication; even Dickens could not resist her appeal, and in a letter to Forster (dated July 1843) he wrote: "I have heard, as you have, from Lady Blessington, for whose behalf I have this morning penned the lines I send you herewith. But I have only done so to excuse myself, for I have not the least idea of their suiting her; and I hope she will send them back to you for *The Examiner*." Lady Blessington, however, decided to retain the thoughtful little poem, which was referred to in the London *Review* (twenty-three years later) as "a graceful and sweet apologue, reminding one of the manner of Hood". The theme of the poem, which Forster describes as "a clever and pointed parable in verse", was afterwards satirized in Chadband (*Bleak House*), and in the idea of religious conversion through the agency of "moral pocket handkerchiefs".

A Word in Season

They have a superstition in the East,
   That Allah, written on a piece of paper,
Is better unction than can come of priest,
   Of rolling incense and of lighted taper:
Holding, that any scrap which bears that name,
   In any characters, its front imprest on,
Shall help the finder through the purging flame,
   And give his toasted feet a place to rest on.

Accordingly, they make a mighty fuss
   With ev'ry wretched tract and fierce oration,
And hoard the leaves – for they are not, like us,
   A highly civilized and thinking nation:
And, always stooping in the miry ways,
   To look for matter of this earthy leaven,
They seldom, in their dust-exploring days,
   Have any leisure to look up to Heaven.

So have I known a country on the earth,
   Where darkness sat upon the living waters,
And brutal ignorance, and toil, and dearth
   Were the hard portion of its sons and daughters:

And yet, where they who should have ope'd the door
   Of charity and light, for all men's finding,
Squabbled for words upon the altar floor,
   And rent the Book, in struggles for the binding.

The gentlest man among these pious Turks,
   God's living image ruthlessly defaces;
Their best high-church man, with no faith in works,
   Bowstrings the Virtues in the marketplaces;
The Christian Pariah, whom both sects curse
   (They curse all other men, and curse each other),
Walks thro' the world, not very much the worse –
   Does all the good he can, and loves his brother.

Verses from
The *Daily News*
1846

The *Daily News*, it will be remembered, was founded in January, 1846, by Charles Dickens, who officiated as its first editor. He soon sickened of the mechanical drudgery appertaining to the position, and resigned his editorial functions the following month. From 21st January to 2nd March he contributed to its columns a series of "Travelling Sketches", afterwards reprinted in volume form as *Pictures from Italy*. He also availed himself of the opportunity afforded him, by his association with that newspaper, of once more taking up the cudgels against the Tories, and, as in the case of *The Examiner*, his attack was conveyed through the medium of some doggerel verses. These were entitled 'The British Lion – A New Song, but an Old Story', to be sung to the tune of 'The Great Sea-Snake'. They bore the signature of "Catnach", the famous ballad-singer, and were printed in the *Daily News* of 24th January 1846.

Three weeks later some verses of a totally different character appeared in the columns of the *Daily News*, signed in full "Charles Dickens". One Lucy Simpkins, of Bremhill (or Bremble), a parish in Wiltshire, had just previously addressed a night meeting of the wives of agricultural labourers in that county, in support of a petition for free trade, and her vigorous speech on that occasion inspired Dickens to write 'The Hymn of the Wiltshire Labourers', thus offering an earnest protest against oppression. Concerning the 'Hymn', a writer in a recent issue of *Christmas Bells* observes: "It breathes in every line the teaching of the Sermon on the Mount, the love of the All-Father, the redemption by His Son, and that love to God and man on which hang all the law and the prophets."

The British Lion
A New Song, but an Old Story
(Tune – 'The Great Sea Snake')

Oh, p'r'aps you may have heard, and if not, I'll sing
   Of the British Lion free,
That was constantly a-going for to make a spring
   Upon his en-e-my;
But who, being rather groggy at the knees,
   Broke down, always, before;
And generally gave a feeble wheeze
   Instead of a loud roar.
     Right toor rol, loor rol, fee faw fum,
      The British Lion bold!
     That was always a-going for to do great things,
      And was always being "sold"!

He was carried about in a carawan,
   And was show'd in country parts,
And they said, "Walk up! Be in time! He can
   Eat Corn-Law Leagues like tarts!"
And his showmen, shouting there and then,
   To puff him didn't fail,

And they said, as they peep'd into his den,
    "Oh, don't he wag his tail!"

Now, the principal keeper of this poor old beast,
    Wan Humbug was his name,
Would once every day stir him up – at least –
    And wasn't that a game!
For he hadn't a tooth, and he hadn't a claw,
    In that "struggle" so "sublime";
And, however sharp they touch'd him on the raw,
    He couldn't come up to time.

And this, you will observe, was the reason why
    Wan Humbug, on weak grounds,
Was forced to make believe that he heard his cry
    In all unlikely sounds.
So, there wasn't a bleat from an Essex Calf,
    Or a duke, or a lordling slim;
But he said, with a wery triumphant laugh,
    "I'm blest if that ain't him."

At length, wery bald in his mane and tail,
    The British Lion growed:
He pined, and declined, and he satisfied
    The last debt which he owed.
And when they came to examine the skin,

It was a wonder sore,
To find that the an-i-mal within
Was nothing but a Boar!
Right toor rol, loor rol, fee faw fum,
The British Lion bold!
That was always a-going for to do great things,
And was always being "sold"!

Catnach.

The Hymn of the Wiltshire Labourers

"Don't you all think that we have a great need to Cry to our God to put it in the hearts of our greassous Queen and her Members of Parlerment to grant us free bread!"

— Lucy Simpkins, *at Bremhill.*

O God! who by Thy prophet's hand
   Didst smite the rocky brake,
Whence water came, at Thy command,
   Thy people's thirst to slake;
Strike, now, upon this granite wall,
   Stern, obdurate and high;
And let some drops of pity fall
   For us who starve and die!

The God who took a little child
   And set him in the midst,
And promised him His mercy mild,
   As, by Thy Son, Thou didst:
Look down upon our children dear,
   So gaunt, so cold, so spare,
And let their images appear
   Where lords and gentry are!

O God! teach them to feel how we,
　　When our poor infants droop,
Are weakened in our trust in Thee,
　　And how our spirits stoop;
For, in Thy rest, so bright and fair,
　　All tears and sorrows sleep:
And their young looks, so full of care,
　　Would make Thine angels weep!

The God who with His finger drew
　　The judgement coming on,
Write, for these men, what must ensue,
　　Ere many years be gone!
O God! whose bow is in the sky,
　　Let them not brave and dare,
Until they look (too late) on high,
　　And see an Arrow there!

O God, remind them! In the bread
　　They break upon the knee,
These sacred words may yet be read,
　　"In memory of Me"!
O God! remind them of His sweet
　　Compassion for the poor,
And how He gave them Bread to eat,
　　And went from door to door!

Charles Dickens.

New Song,
Lines Addressed to Mark Lemon
1849

Dickens, like Silas Wegg, would sometimes "drop into poetry" when writing to intimate friends, as, for example, in a letter to Maclise, the artist, which began with a parody of Byron's lines to Thomas Moore:

> My foot is in the house,
> My bath is on the sea,
> And, before I take a souse,
> Here's a single note to thee.

A more remarkable instance of his propensity to indulge in parody of this kind is to be found in a letter addressed to Mark Lemon in the spring of 1849. The novelist was then enjoying a holiday with his wife and daughters at Brighton, whence he wrote to Lemon (who had been ill), pressing him to pay them a visit. After commanding him to "get a clean pocket handkerchief ready for the close of *Copperfield* No. 3 – 'simple and quiet, but very natural and touching' – *Evening Bore*", Dickens invites his friend in lines headed "New Song" and signed "T. Sparkler", the effusion also bearing the signatures of other members of the family party – Catherine Dickens, Annie Leech, Georgina Hogarth, Mary Dickens, Katie Dickens and John Leech.

New Song
(Tune – 'Lesbia Hath a Beaming Eye')

I

Lemon is a little hipped,
  And this is Lemon's true position –
He is not pale, he's not white-lipped,
  Yet wants a little fresh condition.
Sweeter 'tis to gaze upon
  Old ocean's rising, falling billers,
Than on the houses every one
    That form the street called Saint Anne's Willers!
    Oh, my Lemon, round and fat,
      Oh, my bright, my right, my tight 'un,
    Think a little what you're at –
Don't stay at home, but come to Brighton!

II

Lemon has a coat of frieze,
  But all so seldom Lemon wears it,
That it is a prey to fleas,
  And ev'ry moth that's hungry tears it.
Oh, that coat's the coat for me,
  That braves the railway sparks and breezes,

Leaving ev'ry engine free
   To smoke it, till its owner sneezes!
     Then, my Lemon round and fat,
       L., my bright, my right, my tight 'un,
     Think a little what you're at –
       On Tuesday first, come down to Brighton!

                                        T. Sparkler

Wilkie Collins's Play
The Lighthouse
1855

Wilkie Collins composed two powerful dramas for representation at Dickens's residence, Tavistock House, a portion of which had been already adapted for private theatricals, the rooms so converted being described in the bills as "The Smallest Theatre in the World". The first of these plays was called *The Lighthouse*, and the initial performance took place on 19th June 1855. Dickens not only wrote the Prologue and 'The Song of the Wreck', but signally distinguished himself by enacting the part of Aaron Gurnock, a lighthouse-keeper, his clever impersonation recalling Frédéric Lemaître, the only actor he ever tried to take as a model.

With regard to 'The Song of the Wreck', Dickens evidently intended to bestow upon it a different title, for, in a letter addressed to Wilkie Collins during the preparation of the play, he said: "I have written a little ballad for Mary – 'The Story of the Ship's Carpenter and the Little Boy, in the Shipwreck'." The song was rendered by his eldest daughter, Mary (who assumed the role of Phoebe in the play); it was set to the music composed by George Linley for Miss Charlotte Young's pretty ballad, 'Little Nell', of which Dickens became very fond, and which his daughter had been in the habit of singing to him constantly since her childhood. Dr A.W. Ward, Master of Peterhouse, Cambridge University, refers to 'The Song of the Wreck' as "a most successful effort in Cowper's manner".

The Prologue

(Slow music all the time; unseen speaker; curtain down.)

A story of those rocks where doom'd ships come
To cast them wreck'd upon the steps of home,
Where solitary men, the long year through –
The wind their music and the brine their view –
Warn mariners to shun the beacon light;
A story of those rocks is here tonight.
Eddystone Lighthouse!

(Exterior view discovered.)

In its ancient form,
Ere he who built it wish'd for the great storm
That shiver'd it to nothing,* once again
Behold outgleaming on the angry main!
Within it are three men; to these repair
In our frail bark of fancy, swift as air!
They are but shadows, as the rower grim
Took none but shadows in his boat with him.

So be ye shades, and, for a little space,
The real world a dream without a trace.
Return is easy. It will have ye back

Too soon to the old, beaten, dusty track;
For but one hour forget it. Billows, rise;
Blow winds, fall rain, be black, ye midnight skies;
And you who watch the light, arise! arise!
    (*Exterior view rises and discovers the scene.*)

The Song of the Wreck

I

The wind blew high, the waters raved,
  A ship drove on the land,
A hundred human creatures saved
  Kneel'd down upon the sand.
Threescore were drown'd, threescore were thrown
  Upon the black rocks wild,
And thus among them, left alone,
  They found one helpless child.

II

A seaman rough, to shipwreck bred,
  Stood out from all the rest,
And gently laid the lonely head
  Upon his honest breast.
And travelling o'er the desert wide
  It was a solemn joy,
To see them, ever side by side,
  The sailor and the boy.

III

In famine, sickness, hunger, thirst,
  The two were still but one,
Until the strong man droop'd the first

And felt his labours done.
Then to a trusty friend he spake,
   "Across the desert wide,
Oh, take this poor boy for my sake!"
   And kiss'd the child and died.

IV

Toiling along in weary plight
   Through heavy jungle, mire,
These two came later every night
   To warm them at the fire.
Until the captain said one day
   "O seaman, good and kind,
To save thyself now come away,
   And leave the boy behind!"

V

The child was slumbering near the blaze:
   "O captain, let him rest
Until it sinks, when God's own ways
   Shall teach us what is best!"
They watch'd the whiten'd, ashy heap,
   They touch'd the child in vain;
They did not leave him there asleep,
   He never woke again.

Prologue to Wilkie Collins's Play
The Frozen Deep
1856

The second drama written by Wilkie Collins for the Tavistock House Theatre was first acted there in January 1857, and subsequently at the Gallery of Illustration in the presence of Queen Victoria and the royal family. As in the case of *The Lighthouse*, the play had the advantage of a Prologue in rhyme by Charles Dickens, who again electrified his audiences by marvellous acting, the character of Richard Wardour (a young naval officer) being selected by him for representation. The Prologue was recited at Tavistock House by John Forster, and at the public performances of the play by Dickens himself.

It is not generally known that a by no means inconsiderable portion of the drama was composed by Dickens, as testified by the original manuscripts of the play and of the promptbook, which contain numerous additions and corrections in his handwriting. These manuscripts, by the way, realized three hundred pounds at Sotheby's in 1890.

The main idea of *A Tale of Two Cities* was conceived by Dickens when performing in *The Frozen Deep*. "A strong desire was upon me then," he writes in the preface to the story, "to embody it in my own person; and I traced out in my fancy the state of mind of which it would necessitate the presentation to an observant spectator, with particular care and interest. As the idea became familiar to me, it gradually shaped itself into its present form. Throughout its execution it has had complete possession of me: I have so far verified what is done and suffered in these pages, as that I have certainly done and suffered it all myself."

Prologue to
The Frozen Deep

(*Curtain rises; mists and darkness; soft music throughout.*)

One savage footprint on the lonely shore
Where one man listen'd to the surge's roar,
Not all the winds that stir the mighty sea
Can ever ruffle in the memory.
If such its interest and thrall, oh, then
Pause on the footprints of heroic men,
Making a garden of the desert wide
Where Parry conquer'd death and Franklin died.*

To that white region where the lost lie low,
Wrapt in their mantles of eternal snow –
Unvisited by change, nothing to mock
Those statues sculptured in the icy rock,
We pray your company; that hearts as true
(Though nothings of the air) may live for you;
Nor only yet that on our little glass
A faint reflection of those wilds may pass,

But that the secrets of the vast Profound
Within us, an exploring hand may sound,
Testing the region of the ice-bound soul,
Seeking the passage at its northern pole,
Softening the horrors of its wintry sleep,
Melting the surface of that "Frozen Deep".

Vanish, ye mists! But ere this gloom departs,
And to the union of three sister arts
We give a winter evening, good to know
That in the charms of such another show,
That in the fiction of a friendly play,
The Arctic sailors, too, put gloom away,
Forgot their long night, saw no starry dome,
Hail'd the warm sun, and were again at Home.

Vanish, ye mists! Not yet do we repair
To the still country of the piercing air;
But seek, before we cross the troubled seas,
An English hearth and Devon's waving trees.

A Child's Hymn
from *The Wreck of the Golden Mary*
1856

The Christmas number of *Household Words* for 1856 is especially noteworthy as containing the Hymn of five verses which Dickens contributed to the second chapter. This made a highly favourable impression, and a certain clergyman, the Rev. R.H. Davies, was induced to express to the editor of *Household Words* his gratitude to the author of these lines for having thus conveyed to innumerable readers such true religious sentiments. In acknowledging the receipt of the letter, Dickens observed that such a mark of approval was none the less gratifying to him because he was himself the author of the Hymn. "There cannot be many men, I believe," he added, "who have a more humble veneration for the New Testament, or a more profound conviction of its all-sufficiency, than I have. If I am ever (as you tell me I am) mistaken on this subject, it is because I discountenance all obtrusive professions of and tradings in religion as one of the main causes why real Christianity has been retarded in this world; and because my observation of life induces me to hold in unspeakable dread and horror those unseemly squabbles about the letter which drive the spirit out of hundreds of thousands." – *Vide* Forster's *Life of Charles Dickens*, Book XI, Chapter III.

A Child's Hymn

Hear my prayer, O heavenly Father,
   Ere I lay me down to sleep;
Bid Thy angels, pure and holy,
   Round my bed their vigil keep.

My sins are heavy, but Thy mercy
   Far outweighs them, every one;
Down before Thy cross I cast them.
   Trusting in Thy help alone.

Keep me through this night of peril
   Underneath its boundless shade;
Take me to Thy rest, I pray Thee,
   When my pilgrimage is made.

None shall measure out Thy patience
   By the span of human thought;
None shall bound the tender mercies
   Which Thy Holy Son has bought.

Pardon all my past transgressions,
   Give me strength for days to come;
Guide and guard me with Thy blessing
   Till Thy angels bid me home.

Note on the Text

The text of the poems and the introductory commentaries by F.G. Kitton (1856–1904) is taken from *The Poems and Verses of Charles Dickens* (New York and London: Harper & Brothers, 1903). The notes below, with the exception of the note to p. 99, have been newly added for the present edition. The spelling and punctuation have been standardized, modernized and made consistent throughout.

Notes

p. 57, *Argus*: A reference to Argus Panoptes, a giant with a hundred eyes, in Greek myth.

p. 58, *William Pitt*: A reference to William Pitt the Younger (1759–1806), who became Prime Minister at the young age of twenty-four.

p. 63, *Peter Pindar*: The pseudonym of John Wolcot (1738–1819), who wrote satirical poems, notably about members of the Royal Academy.

p. 63, *Sir Martin*: Sir Martin Archer Shee (1769–1850), a British portrait painter and president of the Royal Academy.

p. 63, *Maclise*: Daniel Maclise (1806–70), a London-based Irish portrait painter.

p. 63, *Chalon*: Alfred Edward Chalon (1780–1860), a London-based Swiss portrait painter who was a favourite among high-society patrons.

p. 63, *Landseer*: Sir Edwin Henry Landseer (1802–73), a painter and sculptor, famous for his depictions of animals.

- p. 63, *Sibthorp*: Charles de Laet Waldo Sibthorp (1783–55), usually referred to as Colonel Sibthorp, was a famously reactionary Tory politician of the time.
- p. 63, *Arcades ambo*: "Both Arcadians" (Latin). Originally from Virgil's *Eclogues*, this phrase denotes two people of the same background or profession.
- p. 64, *Lord Chamberlain Howe*: Richard William Penn Curzon-Howe, 1st Earl Howe (1796–1870) was Lord Chamberlain to the Queen at the time.
- p. 64, *Joseph Hume*: Joseph Hume (1777–1855) was a Scottish MP for the Radical Party.
- p. 65, *Joseph Surface*: The villain in the play *The School for Scandal* (1777) by Richard Brinsley Sheridan (1751–1816).
- p. 65, *Frost*: John Frost (1784–1877) was one of the leaders of the Chartist movement of the 1830s and 1840s, which advocated democratic political reform.
- p. 65, *Thistlewood, Despard*: Arthur Thistlewood (1774–1820) and Edward Marcus Despard (1751–1803), two famous conspirators.
- p. 99, *he who built it… to nothing*: When Winstanley had brought his work to completion, he is said to have expressed himself so satisfied as to its strength, that he only wished he might be there in the fiercest storm that ever blew. His wish was gratified, and, contrary to his expectations, both he and the building were swept completely away by a furious tempest which burst along the coast in November 1703 (F.G. KITTON'S NOTE).
- p. 107, *Where Parry conquer'd death and Franklin died*: William Edward Parry (1790–1855) and John Franklin (1786–1847) were both leaders of Arctic explorations; the latter lost his life (along with his entire crew) on a mission to navigate the North-west Passage.

Extra Material

on

Charles Dickens's

Poems

Charles Dickens's Life

Charles John Huffam Dickens was born in Portsmouth on 7th *First Years*
February 1812 to John Dickens and Elizabeth Dickens, née Barrow.
His father worked as a navy payroll clerk at the local dockyard,
before transferring and moving his family to London in 1814,
and then to Kent in 1817. It seems that this period possessed an
idyllic atmosphere for ever afterwards in Dickens's mind. Much
of his childhood was spent reading and rereading the books in
his father's library, which included *Robinson Crusoe*, *The Vicar
of Wakefield*, *Don Quixote*, Fielding, Smollett and the *Arabian
Nights*. He was a promising, prize-winning pupil at school, and
generally distinguished by his cleverness, sensitivity and enthusi-
asm, although unfortunately this was tempered by his frail and
sickly constitution. It was at this time that he also had his first
experience of what would become one of the abiding passions
in his life: the theatre. Sadly, John Dickens's finances had become
increasingly unhealthy, a situation which was worsened when he
was transferred to London in 1822. This relocation, which en-
tailed a termination in his schooling, distressed Charles, though
he slowly came to be fascinated with the teeming, squalid streets
of London.

In London, however, family finances continued to plummet *Bankruptcy*
until the Dickenses were facing bankruptcy. A family connection, *and the*
James Lamert, offered to employ Charles at the Warren's Blacking *Warehouse*
Warehouse, which he was managing, and Dickens started working
there in February 1824. He spent between six months and a year
there, and the experience would prove to have a profound and
lasting effect on him. The work was drudgery – sealing and label-
ling pots of black paste all day – and his only companions were
uneducated working-class boys. His discontent at the situation was
compounded by the fact that his talented older sister was sent to
the Royal Academy of Music, while he was left in the warehouse.

John Dickens was finally arrested for debt and taken to Mar-
shalsea Prison in Southwark on 20th February 1824, his wife and

children (excluding Charles) moving in with him in order to save money. Meanwhile, Charles found lodgings with an intimidating old lady called Mrs Roylance (on whom he apparently modelled Mrs Pipchin in *Dombey and Son*) in Little College Street, later moving to Lant Street in Borough, which was closer to the prison. At the end of May 1824, John Dickens was released, and gradually paid off creditors as he attempted to start a new life for himself and his family. However, for some time afterwards Charles reluctantly pursued his employment at the blacking factory, as it seems his mother was unwilling to take him out of it, and even tried to arrange for him to return after he did leave. It appears that he was only removed from the warehouse after his father had quarrelled with James Lamert. The stint at the blacking factory was so profoundly humiliating for Dickens that throughout his life he apparently never mentioned this experience to any of those close to him, revealing it only in a fragment of a memoir written in 1848 and presented to his biographer John Forster: "No words can express the secret agony of my soul as I sunk into this companionship, compared these everyday associates with those of my happier childhood, and felt my early hopes of growing up to be a learned and distinguished man crushed in my breast."

School and Work in London

Fortunately he was granted some respite from hard labour when he was sent to be educated at the Wellington House Academy on Hampstead Road. Although the standard of teaching he received was apparently mediocre, the two years he spent at the school were idyllic compared to his warehouse experience, and Charles took advantage of them by making friends his own age and participating in school drama. Regrettably he had to leave the Academy in 1827, when the family finances were in turmoil once again. He found employment as a junior clerk in a solicitor's office, a job that, although routine and somewhat unfulfilling, enabled Dickens to become familiar with the ways of the London courts and the jargon of the legal profession – which he would later frequently lampoon in his novels. On reaching his eighteenth birthday, Dickens enrolled as a reader at the British Museum, determined to make up for the inadequacies of his education by studying the books in its collection, and taught himself shorthand in the hope of taking on journalistic work.

In less than a year he set himself up as a freelance law reporter, initially covering the civil law courts known as Doctors' Commons – which he did with some brio, though he found it slightly tedious – and in 1831 advanced to the press gallery of the House of Commons. His reputation as a reporter was growing steadily, and in 1834 he joined the staff of the *Morning Chronicle*, one of the leading daily newspapers. During this period, he observed and commented on some of the most socially significant debates of the time, such as the Reform Act of 1832, the Factory Act of 1833 and the Poor Law Amendment Act of 1834.

In 1829, he fell in love with the flirtatious and beautiful Maria Beadnell, the daughter of a wealthy banker, and he seems to have remained fixated on her for several years, although she rebuffed his advances. This disappointment spurred him on to achieve a higher station in life, and – after briefly entertaining the notion of becoming an actor – he threw himself into his work and wrote short stories in his spare time, which he had published in magazines, although without pay.

First Love

Soon enough his work for the *Morning Chronicle* was not limited to covering parliamentary matters: in recognition of his capacity for descriptive writing, he was encouraged to write reviews and sketches, and cover important meetings, dinners and election campaigns – which he reported on with enthusiasm. Written under the pseudonym "Boz", his sketches on London street life – published in the *Morning Chronicle* and then also in its sister paper, the *Evening Chronicle* – were highly rated and gained a popular following. Things were also looking up in Dickens's personal life, as he fell in love with Catherine Hogarth, the daughter of the editor of the *Evening Chronicle*: they became engaged in May 1835, and married on 2nd April 1836 at St Luke's Church in Chelsea, honeymooning in Kent afterwards. At this time his literary career began to gain momentum: first his writings on London were compiled under the title *Sketches by Boz* and printed in an illustrated two-volume edition, and then, just a few days before his wedding, *The Pickwick Papers* began to be published in monthly instalments – becoming the best-selling serialization since Lord Byron's *Childe Harold's Pilgrimage*.

Marriage and First Major Publication

At the end of 1836, Dickens resigned from the *Morning Chronicle* to concentrate on his literary endeavours, and met John Forster, who was to remain a lifelong friend. He helped Dickens to manage the business and legal side of his life, as well as acting as a trusted literary adviser and biographer. Forster's acumen for resolving complex situations was particularly welcome at this point, since, following the resounding success of *The Pickwick Papers*, Dickens had over-committed himself to a number of projects, with newspapers and publishers eager to capitalize on the latest literary sensation, and the deals and payments agreed no longer reflected his stature as an author.

Success

In January 1837, Catherine gave birth to the couple's first child, also called Charles, which prompted the young Dickens family to move from their lodgings in Furnival's Inn in Holborn to a house on 48 Doughty Street. The following month *Oliver Twist* started appearing in serial form in *Bentley's Miscellany*, which lifted the author's name to new heights. This period of domestic bliss and professional fulfilment was tragically interrupted when Catherine's sister Mary suddenly died in May at the age of seventeen. Dickens was devastated and had to interrupt work on *The Pickwick Papers* and *Oliver Twist*; this event would have a deep impact on his world view and his art. But his literary productivity would soon continue unabated; hot on the tail of *Oliver Twist* came *Nicholas Nickleby* (1838–39) and *The Old Curiosity Shop* (1840–41). By this stage, he was the leading author of the day, frequenting high society and meeting luminaries such as his idol, Thomas Carlyle. Consequently he moved to a grand Georgian house near Regent's Park, and frequently holidayed in a house in Broadstairs in Kent.

Whereas his previous novels had all more or less followed his successful formula of comedy, melodrama and social satire, Dickens opted for a different approach for his next major work, *Barnaby Rudge*, a purely historical novel. He found the writing of this book particularly arduous, so he decided that after five years of intensive labour he needed a sabbatical, and persuaded his publishers Chapman and Hall to grant him a year's leave with a monthly advance of £150 on his future earnings. During this year he would visit America and keep a notebook on his travels, with a view to getting it published on his return.

First Visit to America Dickens journeyed by steamship to Halifax, Nova Scotia, accompanied by his wife, in January 1842, and the couple would spend almost five months travelling around North America, visiting cities such as Boston, New York, Philadelphia, Cincinnati, Louisville, Toronto and Montreal. He was greeted by crowds of enthusiastic well-wishers wherever he went, and met countless important figures such as Henry Wadsworth Longfellow, Edgar Allan Poe and President John Tyler, but after the initial exhilaration of this fanfare he found it exhausting and overwhelming. The trip also brought about its share of disillusionment: having cherished romantic dreams of America being free from the corruption and snobbery of Europe, he was increasingly appalled by certain aspects of the New World, such as slavery, the treatment of prisoners and, perhaps most of all, the refusal of America to sign an international copyright agreement to prevent his works being pirated in America. He wrote articles and made speeches condemning these practices, which resulted in a considerable amount of press hostility.

Having returned to England in the summer of 1842, he published his record of the trip under the title of *American Notes* and the first instalment of *Martin Chuzzlewit* later that year. Unfortunately neither of the two were quite as successful as he or his publishers would have hoped, although Dickens believed *Martin Chuzzlewit* (1842–44) was his finest work to date. During this period, Dickens started taking a greater interest in political and social issues, particularly in the treatment of children employed in mines and factories, and in the "ragged school" movement, which provided free education for destitute children. He became acquainted with the millionaire philanthropist Angela Burdett-Coutts, and persuaded her to give financial support to a school in London. In 1843, he decided to write a seasonal tale which would highlight the plight of the poor, publishing *A Christmas Carol* to great popular success in December 1843. The following year Dickens decided to leave Chapman and Hall, as his relations with them had become increasingly strained, and persuaded his printer Bradbury and Evans to become his new publisher.

Back Home

In July 1844 Dickens relocated his entire family to Genoa in order to escape London and find new sources of inspiration – and also because life in Italy was considerably cheaper. Dickens, although at first taken aback by the decay of the Ligurian capital, appears to have been fascinated by this new country and a quick learner of its language and customs. He did not write much there, apart from another Christmas book, *The Chimes*, the publication of which occasioned a brief return to London. In all the Dickenses remained in Italy for a year, travelling around the country for three months in early 1845, before returning to England in July of that year.

Move to Genoa

In Italy, he discovered that he was apparently able mesmerically to alleviate the condition of Augusta de la Rue, the wife of a Swiss banker, who suffered from anxiety and nervous spasms. This treatment required him to spend a lot of time alone with her, and unsurprisingly Catherine was not best pleased by this turn of events. She was also worn out by the burden of motherhood: they were becoming a large family, and would eventually have a total of ten children. Catherine's sister Georgina therefore began to help out with the children. Georgina was in many ways similar to Mary, whose death had so devastated Dickens, and she became involved with Dickens's various projects.

Back in London, Dickens took part in amateur theatrical productions, and took on the task of editing the *Daily News*, a new national newspaper owned by Bradbury and Evans. However, he had severely underestimated the work involved in editing the publication and resigned after seventeen issues, though he did continue to write contributions, including a series of 'Travelling Letters' – later collected in *Pictures from Italy* (1846).

More Travels Abroad   Perhaps to escape the aftermath of his resignation from the *Daily News* and to focus on composing his next novel, Dickens moved his family to Lausanne in Switzerland. He enjoyed the clean, quiet and beautiful surroundings, as well as the company of the town's fellow English expatriates. He also managed to write fiction: another Christmas tale entitled *The Battle of Life* and, more significantly, the beginning of *Dombey and Son*, which began serialization in September 1846 and was an immediate success.

It was also at this point that his publisher launched a series of cheap editions of his works, in the hope of tapping into new markets. Dickens returned to London, and resumed his normal routine of socializing, amateur theatricals, letter-writing and public speaking, and also became deeply involved in charitable work, such as setting up and administering a shelter for homeless women, which was funded by Miss Burdett-Coutts. *The Haunted Man*, another Christmas story, appeared in 1848, and was followed by his next major novel, *David Copperfield* (1849–50), which received rapturous critical acclaim.

Household Words   *Household Words* was set up at this time, a popular magazine founded and edited by Dickens himself. The magazine contained fictional work by not only Dickens, but also contributors such as Gaskell and Wilkie Collins, and articles on social issues. Dickens continued with his amateur theatricals, which proved a welcome distraction, since Catherine was quite seriously ill, as was his father, who died shortly afterwards. This was followed by the sudden death of his eight-month-old daughter Dora.

The Dickenses moved house again in November 1851, this time to Tavistock House in Tavistock Square. Since it was in a dilapidated state, renovation was necessary, and Dickens personally supervised every detail of this, from the installation of new plumbing to the choice of wallpaper. *Bleak House* (1852–53), his next publication, sold well, though straight after finishing it, Dickens was in desperate need of a break. He went on holiday in France with his family, and then toured Italy with Wilkie Collins and the painter Augustus Egg. After his return to London, Dickens gave a series of public readings to larger audiences than he had been accustomed to. Dickens's histrionic talents thrived in this context and the readings were a triumph, encouraging the author to repeat the exercise throughout his career – indeed, this became a lucrative venture, with Dickens employing his friend Arthur Smith as his booking agent.

During this period Dickens's stance on current politics and society became increasingly critical, which manifested itself in the numerous satirical essays he penned and the darker, more trenchant outlook of *Bleak House* and the two novels that followed, *Hard Times* (1854) and *Little Dorrit* (1855–57). In March 1856, Dickens bought Gad's Hill Place, near Rochester, for use as a country home. He had admired it during childhood country walks with his father, who had told him he might eventually own it if he were very hard-working and persevering.

However, this acquisition of a permanent home was not accompanied by domestic felicity, as by this point Dickens's marriage was in crisis. Relations between Dickens and his wife had been worsening for some time, but it all came to a head when he became acquainted with a young actress by the name of Ellen Ternan and apparently fell in love with her. The affair may never have been consummated, but Dickens involved himself with Ellen and her family's life to an extent which alarmed Catherine, just as she had been alarmed by the excessive attentions he had paid to Mme de la Rue in Genoa. Soon enough, Dickens moved into a separate bedroom in their house, and in May 1858, Dickens and his wife formally separated. This gave rise to a flurry of speculation, including rumours that Dickens was involved in a relationship with the young actress, or even worse, his sister-in-law, Georgina Hogarth, who had opted to continue living with Dickens instead of with her sister. It seemed that some of these allegations may have originated from the Hogarths, his wife's immediate family, and Dickens reacted to this by forcing them to sign a retraction, and by issuing a public statement – against his friends' advice – in *The Times* and *Household Words*. Furthermore, in August of that year one of Dickens's private letters was leaked to the press, which placed the blame for the breakdown of their marriage entirely on Catherine's shoulders, accused her of being a bad mother and insinuated that she was mentally unstable. After some initial protests, Catherine made no further effort to defend herself, and lived a quiet life until her death twenty years later. She apparently never met Dickens again, but never stopped caring about him, and followed his career and publications assiduously.

This conflict in Dickens's personal affairs also had an effect on his professional life: in 1859 the author fell out with Bradbury and Evans after they had refused to run another statement about his private life in one of their publications, the satirical magazine

The End of the Marriage

All the Year Round

Punch. This led him to transfer back to Chapman and Hall and to found a new weekly periodical *All the Year Round*. His first contribution to the magazine was his highly successful second historical novel, *A Tale of Two Cities* (1859), an un-Dickensian work in that it was more or less devoid of comical and satirical elements. *All the Year Round* – which focused more on fiction and less on journalistic pieces than its predecessor – maintained very healthy circulation figures, especially as the second novel to be serialized was the tremendously popular *The Woman in White* by Wilkie Collins, who became a regular collaborator. Dickens also arranged with the New York publisher J.M. Emerson & Co. for his journal to appear across the Atlantic. In December 1860, Dickens began to serialize what would become one of his best-loved novels, the deeply autobiographical *Great Expectations* (1860–61).

Our Mutual Friend   Between the final instalment of *Great Expectations* and the first instalment of his next and final completed novel, *Our Mutual Friend*, there was an uncharacteristically long three-year gap. This period was marked by two deaths in the family in 1863: that of his mother – which came as a relief more than anything, as she had been declining into senility for some time, and Dickens's feeling for her were ambivalent at best – and that of his second son, Walter – for whom Dickens grieved much more deeply. He chewed over ideas for *Our Mutual Friend* for at least two years and only began seriously composing it in early 1864, with serialization beginning in May. Although the book is now widely considered a masterpiece, it met with a tepid reception at the time, as readers did not entirely understand it.

Staplehurst Train Disaster   On 9th June 1865, Dickens experienced a traumatic incident: travelling back from France with Ellen Ternan and her mother, he was involved in a serious railway accident at Staplehurst, in which ten people lost their lives. Dickens was physically unharmed, but nevertheless profoundly affected by it, having spent hours tending the dying and injured with brandy. He drew on the experience in the writing of one of his best short stories, 'The Signalman'.

Final Years   Following the success of his public readings in Britain, Dickens had been contemplating a tour of the United States, and finally embarked on a second trip to America from December 1867 to April 1868. This turned out to be a very lucrative visit, but the exhaustion occasioned by his punishing schedule proved to be disastrous for his health. He began a farewell tour around England in 1868, incorporating a spectacular piece derived from *Oliver Twist*'s scene of Nancy's murder, but was forced to abandon the tour on the instructions of his doctors after he had a stroke in April 1869. Against medical advice, he insisted on giving a series of twelve final readings in London in 1870. These were very well received, many of those who attended commenting that he had never read so well as then. While in London, he had a private audience with Queen Victoria, and met the Prime Minister.

Dickens immersed himself in writing another major novel, *The Mystery of Edwin Drood*, the first six instalments of which were a critical and financial success. Tragically this novel was never to be completed, as Dickens died on 9th June 1870, having suffered a stroke on the previous day. He had wished to be buried in a small graveyard in Rochester, but this was overridden by a nationwide demand that he should be laid to rest in Westminster Abbey. This was done on 14th June 1870, after a strictly private ceremony which he had insisted on in his will. *Death*

Charles Dickens's Works

As seen in the account of his life above, Charles Dickens was an immensely prolific writer, not only of novels but of countless articles, sketches, occasional writings and travel accounts, published in newspapers, magazines and in volume form. Descriptions of his most famous works can be found below.

Sketches by Boz, a revised and expanded collection of Dickens's newspaper pieces, was published in two volumes by John Macrone on 8th February 1836. The book was composed of sketches of London life, manners and society. It was an immediate success, and was praised by critics for the "startling fidelity" of its descriptions. *Sketches by Boz*

The first instalment of Dickens's first serialized novel, *The Pickwick Papers*, appeared in March 1836. Initially Dickens's contributions were subordinate to those of the illustrator Robert Seymour, but as the series continued, this relationship was inverted, with Dickens's writing at the helm. This led to an upsurge in sales, until *The Pickwick Papers* became a fully fledged literary phenomenon, with circulation rocketing to 40,000 by the final instalment in November 1837. The book centres around the Pickwick Club and its founder, Mr Pickwick, who travels around the country with his companions Mr Winkle, Mr Snodgrass and Mr Tupman, and consists of various loosely connected and light-hearted adventures, with hints of the social satire which would pervade his mature fiction. There is no overall plot, as Dickens invented one episode at a time and, reacting to popular feedback, would switch the emphasis to the most successful characters. *The Pickwick Papers*

Oliver Twist

Dickens's first coherently structured novel, *Oliver Twist*, was serialized in *Bentley's Miscellany* from February 1837 to April 1839, with illustrations by the famous caricaturist George Cruikshank. Subtitled *A Parish Boy's Progress*, in reference to Hogarth's *A Rake's Progress* and *A Harlot's Progress* cycles, Dickens tells the story of a young orphan's life and ordeals in London – which had never before been the substance of a novel – as he flees the workhouse and unhappy apprenticeship of his childhood to London, where he falls in with a criminal gang led by the malicious Fagin, before eventually discovering the secret of his origins. *Oliver Twist* publicly addressed issues such as workhouses and child exploitation by criminals – and this preoccupation with social ills and the plight of the downtrodden would become a hallmark of Dickens's fiction.

Nicholas Nickleby

Dickens's next published novel – the serialization of which for a while overlapped with that of *Oliver Twist* – was *Nicholas Nickleby*, which revolves around its eponymous hero – again an impoverished young man, though an older one this time – as he tenaciously overcomes the odds to establish himself in the world. When Nicholas's father dies penniless, the family turn to their uncle Ralph Nickleby for assistance, but he turns out to be a mean-spirited miser, and only secures menial positions for Nicholas and his sister Kate. Nicholas is sent to work in Dotheboys Hall, a dreadful Yorkshire boarding school administered by the schoolmaster Wackford Squeers, while Kate endures a humiliating stint at a London millinery. The plot twists and turns until both end up finding love and a secure position in life. Dickens's satire is more trenchant, particularly with regard to Yorkshire boarding schools, which were notorious at the time. Interestingly, within ten years of *Nicholas Nickleby*'s publication all the schools in question were closed down. Overall though, the tone is jovial and the plot is rambling and entertaining, much in the vein of Dickens's eighteenth-century idols Fielding and Smollett.

The Old Curiosity Shop

The Old Curiosity Shop started out as a piece in the short-lived weekly magazine that Dickens was editing, *Master Humphrey's Clock*, which began publication in April 1840. It was intended to be a miscellany of one-off stories, but as sales were disappointing, Dickens was forced to adapt the 'Personal Adventures of Master Humphrey' into a full-length narrative that would be the most Romantic and fairy-tale-like of Dickens's novels, with some of his greatest humorous passages. The story revolves around Little Nell, a young girl who lives with her grandfather in his eponymous shop, and recounts how the two struggle to release themselves from the grip of the evil usurer dwarf Quilp. By the end of its serialization, circulation had reached the phenomenal figure of 100,000, and Little Nell's death had famously plunged thousands of readers into grief.

As seen above, Dickens took on a different genre for his next major work of fiction, *Barnaby Rudge*: this was a historical novel, addressing the anti-Catholic Gordon riots of 1780, which focused on a village outside London and its protagonist, a simpleton called Barnaby Rudge. The novel was serialized in *Master Humphrey's Clock* from 1840 to 1841, and met with a lukewarm reception from the reading public, who thirsted for more novels in the vein of *The Old Curiosity Shop*.

Barnaby Rudge

Dickens therefore gave up on the historical genre, and began serializing the more picaresque *Martin Chuzzlewit* from December 1842 to June 1844. The book explores selfishness and its consequences: the eponymous protagonist is the grandson and heir of the wealthy Martin Chuzzlewit senior, and is surrounded by relatives eager to inherit his money. But when Chuzzlewit junior finds himself disinherited and penniless, he has to make his own way in the world. Although it was a step forwards in his writing, being the first of his works to be written with a fully predetermined overall design, it sold poorly – partly due to the fact that publishing in general was experiencing a slump in the early 1840s. In a bid to revive sales, Dickens adjusted the plot during the serialization and sent the title character to America – his own recent visit there providing much material.

Martin Chuzzlewit

In 1843, Dickens had the idea of writing a small seasonal Christmas book, which would aim to revive the spirit of the holiday and address the social problems that he was increasingly interested in. The resulting work, *A Christmas Carol*, was a phenomenal success at the time, and the tale and its characters, such as Scrooge, Bob Cratchit and Tiny Tim, have now achieved an iconic status. Thackeray famously praised it as "a national benefit and to every man or woman who reads it a personal kindness". Dickens published four more annual Christmas novellas – *The Chimes*, *The Cricket on the Hearth*, *The Battle of Life* and *The Haunted Man* – which were successful at the time, but did not quite live up to the classic appeal of *A Christmas Carol*. After *The Haunted Man*, Dickens discontinued his Christmas books, but he included annual Christmas stories in his magazines *Household Words* and *All the Year Round*. Each set of these stories usually took the form of a miniature *Arabian Nights*, with a number of unrelated short stories linked together through a frame narrative – typically Dickens wrote the frame narrative, and invited other writers to supply the stories included within it, writing the occasional one of them himself. *The Haunted House* appeared in *All the Year Round* in 1862.

Christmas Books and The Haunted House

Dombey and Son   While living in Lausanne, Dickens composed *Dombey and Son*, which was serialized between October 1846 and April 1848 by Bradbury and Evans with highly successful results. The novel centres on Paul Dombey, the wealthy owner of a shipping company, who desperately wants a son to take over his business after his death. Unfortunately his wife dies giving birth to the longed-for successor, Paul Dombey junior, a sickly child who does not survive long. Although Dombey – who neglects his fatherly responsibilities towards his daughter Florence – is for the most part unsympathetic, he ends up turning a new leaf and becoming a devoted family man. Significantly, this is the first of Dickens's novels for which his working notes survive, from which one can clearly see the great care and detail with which he planned the novel.

David Copperfield   *David Copperfield* (1849–1850) is at once the most personal and the most popular of Dickens's novels. He had tried, probably during 1847–48, to write his autobiography, but, according to his own later account, had found writing about certain aspects, such as his first love for Maria Beadnell, too painful. Instead he chose to transpose autobiographical events into a first-person *Bildungsroman*, *David Copperfield*, which drew on his personal experience of the blacking factory, journalism, his schooling at Wellington House and his love for Maria. Its depiction of the Micawbers owed much to Dickens's own parents. There was great critical acclaim for the novel, and it soon became widely held to be his greatest work.

Bleak House   For his next novel, *Bleak House* (1852–53), Dickens turned his satirical gaze on the English legal system. The focus of the novel is a long-running court case, Jarndyce and Jarndyce, the consequences of which reach from the filthy slums to the landed aristocracy. The scope of the novel may well be the broadest of all of his works, and Dickens also experimented with dual narrators, one in the third person and one in the first. He was well equipped to write on the subject matter due to his experiences as a law clerk and journalist, and his critique of the judiciary system was met with recognition by those involved in it, which helped set the stage for its reform in the 1870s.

Hard Times   *Hard Times* was Dickens's next novel, serialized in *Household Words* between April and August 1854, in which he satirically probed into social and economic issues to a degree not achieved in his other works. Using the infamous characters Thomas Gradgrind and Josiah Bounderby, he attacks utilitarianism, workers' conditions in factories, spurious usage of statistics and fact as opposed to imagination. The story is set in the fictitious northern industrial setting of Coketown, among the workers, school pupils and teachers.

The shortest and most polemical of Dickens's major novels, it sold extremely well on publication, but has only recently been fully accepted into the canon of Dickens's most significant works.

Little Dorrit (1855–57) was also a darkly critical novel, satirizing the shortcomings of the government and society, with institutions such as debtor's prisons – in one of which, as seen above, Dickens's own father had been held – and the fantastically named Circumlocution Office bearing the brunt of Dickens's bile. The plot centres on the romance which develops between the characters of Little Dorrit, a paragon of virtue who has grown up in prison, and Arthur Clennam, a hapless middle-aged man who returns to England to make a living for himself after many years abroad. Although at the time many critics were hostile to the work, taking issue with what they saw as an overly convoluted plot and a lack of humour, sales were outstanding and the novel is now ranked as one of Dickens's finest. *Little Dorrit*

A Tale of Two Cities is the second of Dickens's historical novels, covering the period between 1775 and 1793, from the American Revolution until the middle of the French Revolution. His primary source was Thomas Carlyle's *The French Revolution*. The story is of two men – Charles Darnay and Sydney Carton – who look very similar, though they are utterly different in character, who both love the same woman, Lucie Manette. The opening and closing sentences are among the most famous in literature: "It was the best of times, it was the worst of times." "It is a far, far better thing that I do, than I have ever done; it is a far, far better rest that I go to than I have ever known." *A Tale of Two Cities*

Due to a slump in circulation figures for *All the Year Round*, Dickens brought out his next novel, in December 1860, as a weekly serial in the magazine, instead of having it published in monthly instalments as initially intended. The sales promptly recovered, and the audience and critics were delighted to read the story which some regard as Dickens's greatest ever work, *Great Expectations* (1860–61). On publication, it was immediately acclaimed a masterpiece, and was hugely successful in America as well as England. Like *David Copperfield*, it was written in the first person as a *Bildungsroman*, though this time its protagonist, Pip, was explicitly working class. Graham Greene once commented: "Dickens had somehow miraculously varied his tone, but when I tried to analyse his success, I felt like a colour-blind man trying intellectually to distinguish one colour from another." George Orwell was moved to declare: "Psychologically the latter part of *Great Expectations* is about the best thing Dickens ever did." *Great Expectations*

Our Mutual Friend   Dickens started work on his next novel, *Our Mutual Friend* (1864–65), by 1861 at the latest. It had an unusually long gestation period, and a mixed reception when first published. However, in recent years it has been reappraised as one of his greatest works. It is probably his most challenging and complicated, although some critics, including G.K. Chesterton, have argued that the ending is rushed. It opens with a young man on his way to receive his inheritance, which he can apparently only attain if he marries a beautiful and mercenary girl, Bella Wilfer, whom he has never met. However, before he arrives, a body is found in the Thames, which is identified as being him. So instead the money passes on to the Boffins, the effects of which spread through to various parts of London society.

The Mystery of Edwin Drood   In April 1870, the first instalment of Dickens's last novel, *The Mystery of Edwin Drood*, appeared. It was the culmination of Dickens's lifelong fascination with murderers. It was favourably received, outselling *Our Mutual Friend*, but only six of the projected twelve instalments were published, as Dickens died in June of that year.

There has naturally been much speculation on how the book would have finished, and suggestions as to how it should end. As it stands, the novel is set in the fictional area of Cloisterham, which is a thinly veiled rendering of Rochester. The plot mainly focuses on the choirmaster and opium addict John Jasper, who is in love with Rosa Bud – his pupil and his nephew Edwin Drood's fiancée. The twins Helena and Neville Landless arrive in Cloisterham, and Neville is attracted to Rosa Bud. Neville and Edwin end up having a huge row one day, after which Neville leaves town, and Edwin vanishes. Neville is questioned about Edwin's disappearance, and John Jasper accuses him of murder.

Select Bibliography

Biographies:

Ackroyd, Peter, *Dickens* (London: Sinclair-Stevenson, 1990)

Forster, John, *The Life of Charles Dickens* (London: Cecil Palmer, 1872–74)

James, Elizabeth, *Charles Dickens* (London: British Library, 2004)

Kaplan, Fred, *Dickens: A Biography* (London: Hodder & Stoughton, 1988)

Smiley, Jane, *Charles Dickens* (London: Weidenfeld and Nicolson, 2002)

Additional Recommended Background Material:

Collins, Philip, ed., *Dickens: The Critical Heritage* (London: Routledge & Kegan Paul, 1971)

Fielding, K.J, *Charles Dickens: A Critical Introduction* 2nd ed. (London: Longmans, 1965)

Wilson, Angus, *The World of Charles Dickens* (London: Secker & Warburg, 1970)

On the Web:

dickens.stanford.edu

dickens.ucsc.edu

www.dickensmuseum.com

ALMA CLASSICS

ALMA CLASSICS aims to publish mainstream and lesser-known European classics in an innovative and striking way, while employing the highest editorial and production standards. By way of a unique approach the range offers much more, both visually and textually, than readers have come to expect from contemporary classics publishing.

LATEST TITLES PUBLISHED BY ALMA CLASSICS

www.almaclassics.com